More OOMPH

An ABC Book Celebrating Nature

By Anne Lingelbach
Illustrated by Kim VanDenBerg

Published by Orange Hat Publishing 2020
ISBN 978-1-64538-125-9

Copyrighted © 2020 by Anne Lingelbach
All Rights Reserved
More Oomph: An ABC Book Celebrating Nature
Written by Anne Lingelbach
Illustrated by Kim VanDenBerg

All Rights Reserved. Written permission must be secured from the publisher to use or reproduce any part of this book, except for brief quotations in critical reviews or articles.

For information, please contact:

Orange Hat Publishing
www.orangehatpublishing.com
Waukesha, WI

In honor of my mom and twin brother Jon—both word enthusiasts.

Apricate

Apricate
Verb | (ap-ri-cate)

An English word that means to bask in the sun. It first appeared around 1690.

Example
The young children were building sandcastles while their parents apricated on beach towels.

Bosky

Bosky
Adjective | (bosk-y)

An English word for an area of trees or woods. It dates from 1616.

Example
The small herd of deer felt safe near the bosky on the side of the hill.

Clinkerbell

Clinkerbell
Noun | (clinker-bell)
An archaic word for icicle that originated in Somerset, England.

Example
The sparkling clinkerbells hung from the eaves of the old house.

Daffadowndilly

Daffadowndilly
Noun | (daffa- down-dil-ly)

An English word for daffodil that was used in poetry in 1565.

Example
The sunny daffadowndillies blanketed the front yard of the cottage.

Eventide

Eventide
Noun | (e-ven-tide)
An archaic English word that means evening. It was first used before the 12th century.

Example
At eventide, the forest becomes quiet and peaceful.

Fosse

Fosse
Noun | (faws)

An old English word for ditch or moat that is usually filled with water.

Example
The stately swans were swimming in the fosse surrounding the castle.

Gurfa

Gurfa
Noun | (goo-hr-fah)

An Arabic word for the amount of water that can be scooped up in a hand.

Example
The thirsty traveler sipped a gurfa from the waterhole at the oasis.

Hoppipolla

Hoppipolla
Verb | (hopp-i-polla)
An Icelandic word for jumping into puddles.

Example
After a rainstorm, children of all ages like to hoppipolla.

Ignivomous

Ignivomous
Adjective | (ig-niv-o-mous)
A Latin word for vomiting fire, like a volcano does.

Example
The science students were thrilled when they created an ignivomous volcano.

Jheel

Jheel
Noun | (jee-l)

A word from India that means pond or marsh.

Example
The vegetation in the jheel provides food and shelter for the aquatic animals living there.

Komoreibi

Komoreibi
Noun | (kun-yomi)
A Japanese word to describe the sunlight that filters through leaves of trees.

Example
The komoreibi on an autumn day provides a beautiful photo opportunity.

Lapideous

Lapideous
Adjective | (la-pid-e-ous)
A Latin word that means stony.

Example
The lapideous footpath was slippery after the snowfall.

Mangata

Mangata
Noun | (mo-n-ga-ta)

A Swedish word for the light the moon casts on water that looks like a road.

Example
The campers were in awe when they first saw the mangata over the lake.

Nemophilist

Nemophilist
Noun | (ne-moph-i-list)

A word derived from Ancient Greek that describes someone who loves the woods and visits them often.

Example
The nemophilist enjoyed her weekend walks through the countryside.

Owlery

Owlery
Noun | (owl-ery)
An English word that means a place that owls inhabit.

Example
In the fairytale, the owlery was located in the center of the enchanted forest.

Plash

Plash
Noun | (pla-SH)

An English word that means splash.

Example
The plashing sound of the rain on the roof was relaxing and made the little children sleepy.

Quaggy

Quaggy
Adjective | (Kwagi)

An old English word that means soft, watery soil; muddy, mucky, marshy.

Example
The piglets relished playing in the quaggy area of the barnyard.

Rillet

Rillet
Noun | (ril-it)

An archaic English word that means a small stream.

Example
The rillet flowing alongside the road made a gentle gurgling sound.

Sitzmark

Sitzmark
Noun | (sitz-mark)

This word describes the depression left in the snow by a skier falling backward. It is a made-up word using the German verb for sit (sitzen), and the English noun for an impression (mark).

Example
The first-time skier made a sitzmark as he fell down the small hill.

Twirlblast

Twirlblast
Noun | (twirl-blast)
An old English word for tornado.

Example
The storm chasers warned the public about the approaching twirlblast.

Umbracious

Umbracious
Adjective | (um-bra-geous)
An archaic French word for shady.

Example
The family found an umbracious spot in the park for their picnic.

Varec

Varec
Noun | (var-ec)

A French word for seaweed.

Example
The beach was covered with smelly varec and pieces of driftwood.

Williwaw

Williwaw
Noun | (wil-li-waw)
An old English word first used by sailors to describe a sudden violent wind.

Example
The ship's crew was wary of the dangerous williwaw as they sailed along the mountainous coast.

Xenops

Xenops
Noun | (ze-nops)

A small tree creeping bird that lives in the rainforest.

Example
The xenops forages for insects hiding in the bark of tropical trees.

Yertdrift

Yertdrift
Noun | (yert-drift)

An old Scottish word meaning a snowstorm accompanied by a very strong wind.

Example
In the winter, it is difficult for drivers to travel through yertdrifts on their morning commute to work.

Zepher

Zepher
Noun | (zeph-yr)

An ancient word describing a soft, gentle breeze.

Example
The small child laying in the hammock was rocked to sleep by the zepher.

www.ingramcontent.com/pod-product-compliance
Lightning Source LLC
LaVergne TN
LVHW071026070426
835507LV00002B/42